Tiddlers

The Mermaid's Socks

by Clare De Marco

WITHDRAWN

Illustrated by Steve Brown

W

Notes on the series

TIDDLERS are structured to provide support for children who are starting to read on their own. The stories may also be used for sharing with children.

Starting to read alone can be daunting. **TIDDLERS** help by listing the words in the book for a check before reading, and by providing visual support and repeating words and phrases. These books will both develop confidence and encourage reading and rereading for pleasure.

If you are reading this book with a child, here are a few suggestions:

1. Make reading fun! Choose a time to read when you and the child are relaxed and have time to share the story.
2. Talk about the story before you start reading. Look at the cover and the blurb. What might the story be about? Why might the child like it?
3. Look also at the list of words below – can the child tackle most of the words? Encourage the child to employ a phonics approach to tackling new words by sounding the words out.
4. Encourage the child to retell the story, using the jumbled picture puzzle.
5. Give praise! Remember that small mistakes need not always be corrected.

Here is a list of the words in this story.

Common words:

a	her	she
are	it	these
but	lots	they
could	Mum	up
Dad	not	was
for	of	what
go	on	your
got	said	

Other words:

anything	catching	mermaid
birthday	ears	pick
Bubble	hands	presents
bubbles	hear	princess

Princess Bubble was a mermaid.

4

It was her birthday.

HAP

She got lots of
presents.

"What are these for?"
she said.

"They go on your hands," said Dad.

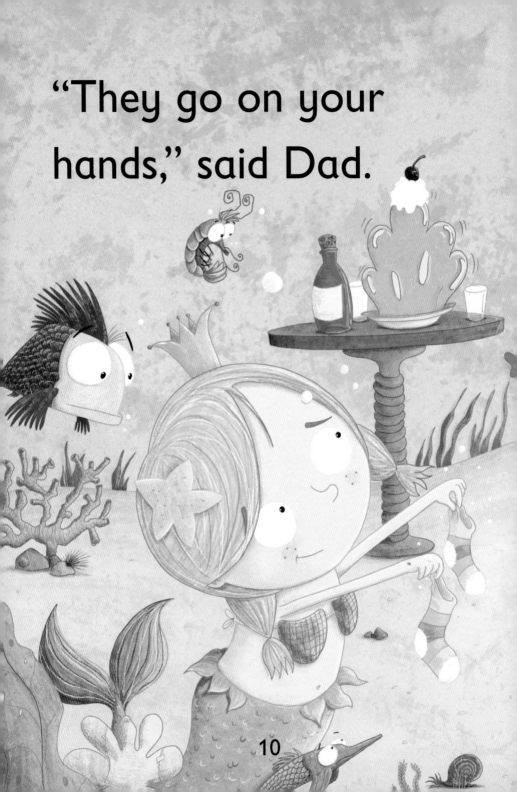

10

11

But Bubble could not
pick anything up.

14

"They go on your ears," said Mum.

But Bubble could not
hear anything.

"Got it!" said Bubble.

19

"They are for catching bubbles!"

Puzzle Time

Can you find these
pictures in the story?

Which pages are the
pictures from?

Turn over for answers!

Answers

The pictures come from these pages:

a. pages 20–21

b. pages 6–7

c. pages 10–11

d. page 3

Franklin Watts
First published in Great Britain in 2016 by
The Watts Publishing Group

Copyright (text) © Clare De Marco 2016
Copyright (illustration) © Steve Brown 2016

The rights of Clare De Marco to be
identified as the author and Steve Brown to
be identified as the illustrator of this Work
have been asserted in accordance with the
Copyright, Designs and Patents Act, 1988.

Series Editor: Jackie Hamley
Series Advisor: Catherine Glavina
Series Designer: Cathryn Gilbert

A CIP catalogue record for this book is
available from the British Library.

ISBN 978 1 4451 4605 8 (hbk)
ISBN 978 1 4451 4607 2 (pbk)
ISBN 978 1 4451 4606 5 (library ebook)

Printed in China

Franklin Watts
An imprint of
Hachette Children's Group
Part of The Watts Publishing Group
Carmelite House
50 Victoria Embankment
London EC4Y 0DZ

An Hachette UK Company
www.hachette.co.uk

www.franklinwatts.co.uk

FSC
www.fsc.org
MIX
Paper from
responsible sources
FSC® C104740